SAFE HARBOR:
LIFE WITH MY OLD LADY

By Quan Jingye

Translated by Denis Mair

New York New Century Press Inc.

作　　者：全京业
译　　者：梅丹理
出版人：洪君植
责任编辑：柳雪花
封面 / 版式设计：龙雁翎

SAFE HARBOR: LIFE WITH MY OLD LADY（诗集）

版权所有 · 翻印必究

出版：纽约新世记出版社
New York New Century Press Inc.
印刷：UCHP Inc.
版次：2018 年 11 月纽约第一版；第一次印刷
定价：9.99 美金
国际书号（ISBN）：ISBN: 978-1-64083-089-9

QUAN, JINGYE

Poet, critic, translator, editor. He was born in Ningan City, Heilongjiang Province in 1959. He is a director of the Korean Chinese National Art Museum of Jilin Province, and the director of the Korean magazine "Doraji" company.

DENIS MAIR

Denis Mair is a poet and translator. His translations include works by Feng Youlan (Hawaii University Press), Wang Meng (Foreign Languages Press), and Shih Chenhua (SUNY Albany Press). He is a co-translator of Forntier Taiwan (Clumbia University Press). His book of poems, Man Cut in Wood, was published by Vally Contemporary Press. He has given lectures on the I CHING at the Temple School of Poetry (Walla Walla).

PROEM

That day I let Junzhi take a look

At ten-or-so of my recent poems

It so happened

Those poems were about my old lady

Junzhi said, "Write some more

We'll publish a little book

And give it to Sister-in-law

In memory of your 34th anniversary"

The two of us were ranting and raving like maniacs

From another room came my sister-in-law's voice

"Don't fool around with unreal things

Buckle down and take care of household tasks

Then you will have everything"

CONTENT

PROEM

Wifey Series #1	SAFE HARBOR	///01
Wifey Series #2	GO BACK TOGETHER	///02
Wifey Series #3	WIFEY PUTS HER LIFEBLOOD INTO COOKING AND DOING MY LAUNDRY	///04
Wifey Series #4	A LEDGER OF SORTS	///05
Wifey Series #5	TOOTHBRUSH	///06
Wifey Series #6	FREQUENT VISITS TO THE KITCHEN	///08
Wifey Series #7	SENSE OF ACCOMPLISHMENT	///09
Wifey Series #8	BLACK PEPPER	///11
Wifey Series #9	NEW YEAR'S DAY	///12
Wifey Series #10	MY INCREDIBLY MOTIVATED WIFE	///13
Wifey Series #11	THE ACTIVE PERIOD OF A HOBBY	///14
Wifey Series #12	AFRAID IT WOULD HAVE A BAD EFFECT	///15
Wifey Series #13	A POLITICALLY-MINDED PERSON	///16
Wifey Series #14	UNEXPECTED INCIDENT	///18
Wifey Series #15	A DIFFERENCE OF OPINION	///19
Wifey Series #16	HANDKERCHIEF	///20
Wifey Series #17	RED PLUM BLOSSOMS IN A PICTURE FRAME	///21
Wifey Series #18	MACHO GAL—VIDEOCASSETTE TAPE	///22

Wifey Series #19	MACHO GAL—STONES	///23
Wifey Series #20	IF YOU'VE BEEN DRINKING, DON'T COME	///25
Wifey Series #21	MACHO GAL—LEVEL 3 ELECTRICIAN	///26
Wifey Series #22	REQUESTS FOR CALLIGRAPHY	///27
Wifey Series #23	FIRST ATTEMPT AT DOING BUSINESS	///28
Wifey Series #24	THE FIRST ACCORDION	///30
Wifey Series #25	FIVE HUNDRED YUAN PER MONTH	///31
Wifey Series #26	CONFIDENCE IN HER OWN JUDGEMENT	///32
Wifey Series #27	TO COOK YOUR MEALS	///33
Wifey Series #28	YOU DON'T OBJECT, DO YOU?	///34
Wifey Series #29	PHONE CONTACTS	///35
Wifey Series #30	"A BIG GUY"	///36
Wifey Series #31	DIARY	///37
Wifey Series #32	THE THOUSAND-CHARACTER CLASSIC	///37
Wifey Series #33	CHOPPING KNIFE	///41
Wifey Series #34	RESUMÉ	///43
Wifey Series #35	RADIUS OF ACTIVITY	///45
Wifey Series #36	A MARVELOUS ENCOUNTER ON TOMB-SWEEPING DAY	///46
Wifey Series #37	IDENTITY	///48
Wifey Series #38	LIFE EXPERIENCE	///49
Wifey Series #39	ON CARING FOR OUR HEALTH	///50
Wifey Series #40	SOMETHING THAT BOTHERS ME	///52
Wifey Series #41	MY OLD LADY CARRIED ME ON HER BACK	///53
Wifey Series #42	MACHO GAL—FACTORY BOSS	///55

Wifey Series #43	IN THE YEARS 2000 AND 2002	///56
Wifey Series #44	WATCH OVER ME	///57
Wifey Series #45	FIRST PIECE OF JEWELRY	///58
Wifey Series #46	ASKING FOR AN EVENING OFF	///59
Wifey Series #47	LIVING ON RICE PORRIGE	///60
Wifey Series #48	TAOBAO	///61
Wifey Series #49	NOW THEY ARE MAKING DEMANDS	///62
Wifey Series #50	VOLUNTEER	///63
Wifey Series #51	SECOND MENOPAUSE	///65
Wifey Series #52	RETAIL VENDING	///66
Wifey Series #53	FILING A LAWSUIT	///67
Wifey Series #54	KOREAN RESTAURANT	///69
Wifey Series #55	EMPLOYMENT AGENCY	///70
Wifey Series #56	WHO FIRED WHOM?	///72
Wifey Series #57	TOO MUCH TO DRINK	///73
Wifey Series #58	ADHERING TO A CODE OF LOYALTY	///74
Wifey Series #59	OLD LADY, LET ME SAY THIS SLOWLY	///76

AFTERWORD   ///81

SAFE HARBOR:

LIFE WITH MY OLD LADY

SAFE HARBOR

Wifey Series #1

I had just written these words: "Now I realize
In every lifetime my mother has been my beloved"

At some point my wife had snuck up from behind
Leaning her head over my shoulder, she asked:
"If your mother is your beloved in every lifetime…
What am I, your goddess?"

Not daring to turn around I asked meekly
"Aren't you my wife in every lifetime?"
My wife looked miffed…She gave me a stare
Then laid back in bed with an accusing look
"Who would have expected you to reach the safe harbor
Of having me as wife!" Before her next sentence was finished
She began snoring with mouth half-open

GO BACK TOGETHER

Wifey Series #2

After a close brush with disaster, I rose and looked admiringly
At my wife who was snoring with mouth open
This safe harbor has grown pudgier…heavier
I thought of her many years ago, slender at forty-plus kilos
Now she weighs sixty kilos…her waist is thicker
Her breasts sag…she used to eat less than two liang of rice
Now she eats big bowls of meat and fish
Just as I was floating on air…surveying my handiwork
My old lady suddenly sat up in bed
"What are you doing? Do you think something is wrong
   with me? You're scaring me
Our daughter isn't worried…my complexion is just a little pale
But tomorrow is Valentine's Day…I'd like to know
Why did you marry me?" I really hadn't thought about it
And I didn't know how to answer
My old lady said, "In insist on finding out today"
I met her stare…in helpless silence
We were deadlocked…the look in her eyes turned frosty
"Well…do you remember what you said
The first time we saw each other?" I asked
"What did I say?" Her gaze softened a bit

"Your exact words were 'Let's go back.' "
"Well, what of it?" Her tone was inquisitive
"Let's go back'…Weren't you asking me to go back
Together with you? That's why I married you"
"Oh, so that's it. Let's…go…back
Let's go back…together"; her voice grew fainter,
As if talking in her sleep…she slumped while finishing her words
And started snoring with her mouth half open

WIFEY PUTS HER LIFEBLOOD INTO COOKING AND DOING MY LAUNDRY

Wifey Series #3

Wifey went away for two months
I rejoiced and hopped in glee
At last I would have two months of liberation

But within a few days
I felt…I felt run-down

Buying vegetables took me over an hour
Cooking meals took two hours in the morning, two in the evening
Straightening up the house took an hour
Washing clothes took an hour
Out of 24 hours in a day
Eight hours got used up, just like that

My better half
On an average
Gives me one third of her life

A LEDGER OF SORTS

Wifey Series #4

At 5:30 am
My old lady gets up, cooks rice, makes breakfast
At seven we eat…after eating
She washes dishes and after that…she polishes my shoes
For half an hour
After that she straightens up the room
When I leave for work at nine
She is only half-finished straightening up

At five in the afternoon I am home
She spends an hour cooking and serving dishes
At six I eat supper…after that
She washes dishes…after that…she washes clothes
Then straightens up the kitchen and laundry room
Takes half an hour…laundering my pants and shirt
At nine o'clock she fools around on her smart phone
Watches a soap opera or call-in show
Within a few minutes
A thread of drool trickles from her open mouth
She falls asleep, snoring as if she owns the world

TOOTHBRUSH

Wifey Series
#5

The day before yesterday
While hurrying to get ready
I used my old lady's toothbrush
—"For a man of almost sixty
You're not particular about hygiene
Maybe it doesn't bother you, but it bothers me
Are you suffering from dementia?
Huh?" She lambasted me
Like a runty grandchild

This morning
I forgot which color
My toothbrush was
—"Is your toothbrush red or is it blue?"
—"We've been married for forty years already
Why keep them separate?
Yours is mine
Mine is yours
Do you object to my age?
Or maybe you've found a hot number outside
Hmm?" She lambasted me

Wifey Series
#5

Like a runty grandchild

FREQUENT VISITS TO THE KITCHEN

Wifey Series #6

Before dinner
While my old lady was busy cooking
I went into the kitchen a few times…
With a skeptical look my daughter said
"The last few days I've seen Daddy
Going into the kitchen frequently"
—"Umm, I'll tell you why
Your mother's cooking smells so good
I want to see how she makes those dishes"
Actually my old lady doesn't add much salt
So her cooking is bland
And she doesn't add MSG…
She claims it causes hair loss
I've endured it for years…these few days
I really could bear it no longer
I went into the kitchen, waiting for a chance
To sneakily add a pinch of salt and MSG

SENSE OF ACCOMPLISHMENT

Wifey Series
#7

A sense of accomplishment
Can lead to disaster

Two months ago my better half
Went to Korea to learn ethnic dance
My wife never admits she's tired, but now
I see her conk out the moment she lays down
I feel sorry for her, so I volunteer
To cook a meal to reward her
You can tell the quality of a person's cooking
By how well they cook pressed beancurd
So of course I cooked pressed beancurd

At lunchtime
My wife raised a slice of beancurd to her moth
Before her tongue even touched it
She exclaimed loudly
—"That's really tasty!
Amazing! It turns out
That you are quite a cook!"

Wifey Series
#7

I felt a special sense of accomplishment
So why do I say
That a sense of accomplishment
Can lead to disaster?

From then on, whenever I'm home
Cooking dinner
Has become an obligation

BLACK PEPPER

Wifey Series
#8

I like the taste of black pepper
My wife doesn't like it
And never adds it to her soups
My only way is to add a pinch in secret

This morning there was no chance
I didn't add it
As we ate breakfast my wife said
"This soup doesn't taste good
I wonder why"

NEW YEAR'S DAY

Wifey Series
#9

New Year's Day, I woke up in the morning
Looked at WeChat messages
Saw that wifey had sent me
Predictions for the year
She sent them out more than once
To her Friends List, her Family List
Her Classmate List, and her Plaza Dance List

"Do you really believe that stuff?"
I knew my wife never went to fortune tellers
She did not believe in them

"Not at all," she said
"But most of it sounds nice
So I forwarded it"

MY INCREDIBLY MOTIVATED WIFE

Wifey Series #10

In 2007 my wife returned

From Qingdao to Jilin

In the past few years

She has gone in for softball, jitterbug

Plaza dancing and ethnic dancing

She has taken part in contests

Gotten a heap of award certificates

She even holds a credential:

"State-Certified Grade 1 Public Fitness Coach"

Luckily I have my poetry writing, such as it is

Otherwise my wife, with a sweep of her arms

Would have me dashing crazily from street to street

THE ACTIVE PERIOD OF A HOBBY

Wifey Series #11

Since her menopause came
The active period of my wife's hobbies
Has been two or three years
But never more than three years

Softball for three years
Jitterbug and plaza dancing
Altogether four years
Korean "elephant hat dance" and "drum dance"
Altogether for three years

After she got tired of them
Before she found another activity to engage in
My wife said to me
"It seems my menopause isn't over"

AFRAID IT WOULD HAVE A BAD EFFECT

Wifey Series #12

One night when I got home

My wife's facial expression was not very nice

"I hope it's not because of me"

"No, it's because of Qingzi

I've done what I could to look out for her

Even so, she opposes me

I guess I won't be having fun with her any more

But that won't do

If I don't take her to have fun

Nobody will have fun with her"

"Since that is your wish…there's nothing to be done about it"

"I just wanted to come home

And complain to you about it

If I complained to other people

I'm afraid it would have a bad effect"

A POLITICALLY-MINDED PERSON

Wifey Series #13

No one is more politically minded than my old lady
The art troupe she founded
Is called Red Star Art Troupe
Her softball team was called
Taichi Wind Softball Team
Each year the clubs she's involved with
Hold an annual meeting
They sum up the previous year's work
And make plans for the coming year
They praise the people who did positive things
And warn those who did negative things
In her written speech for this year's annual meeting
The first paragraph begins like this:
"By making an in-depth study of the spirit
Of the Party's 19th Plenary Session…"
In the last paragraph, the first sentence reads:
—"In the coming year
Hold high the banner
Of socialist thought with Chinese characteristics
To expand cultural consumption…"
What a pity that my wife was hospitalized

Wifey Series
#13

The annual meeting was not held this year

UNEXPECTED INCIDENT

Wifey Series
#14

I sometimes think it's a strange thing
She has not asked for a divorce
From an impractical bookworm like me
I once asked my old lady
—"In over thirty years of marriage
Have you ever known happiness?
Was it when our daughter went to college
Or when we bought a house?"
"Nope…those were things
That were supposed to happen
I was delighted and glad
But I didn't feel that was happiness
There was one time when I really tasted happiness
When we were in Harbin, a road was being repaired
You walked in front and I walked behind
You reached back and grabbed my hand
Very naturally…without turning your head
You just reached back and took my hand
At that moment I felt happiness"

A DIFFERENCE OF OPINION

Wifey Series
#15

In matters of principle, my wife's opinions and mine

Are basically consistent

But there is one issue

Due to the small size of our condo

I remind my wife to throw clothes she doesn't wear

Into our neighborhood's donation box

My wife tells me that the books I've already read

Would be useful if given to others

At home they only take up space

When my wife was away I threw away

Two cartons full of clothes

When I came back from a trip

A few hundred of my books were gone

HANDKERCHIEF

Wifey Series
#16

On the thirteenth anniversary of our marriage
My old lady pulled out a white handkerchief
From somewhere…bearing these lines in bright red

———

You be my thousand-year brass mirror
Let me face you every moment
I'll be the irises of your eyes
Dilating the vividness of your world

———

"Oh my god, could I have written
Something so romantic?"

"Romantic or not…
It's not important if it's well-written or not
The important thing is
How much you put into practice

RED PLUM BLOSSOMS IN A PICTURE FRAME

Wifey Series #17

Photos of all kinds are displayed on the bookshelf
Photos of our daughter, of ourselves, of events
Family portraits taken through the years
One of the frames contains two thumb-sized vases
Each holding red plum blossoms
"This seems useless, let's throw it out"
"No, don't." My wife's attitude was firm
I took a look…those were plum blossoms
My wife had folded and embroidered with her own hands
When my daughter was eight years old
Beneath them was an inscription:
"Among splendors of the capital, the bent pine is lovely
Karma dispelled makes plum-blossoms look jade-like"
Although the lines did not quite fit the image
Our names were embedded there

MACHO GAL—VIDEOCASSETTE TAPE

Wifey Series #18

In the early months of our marriage
We borrowed a video player and cassettes from my work unit
Thinking we could earn a little money
We went to a village to show them
But before we earned money, due to an operating error
The magnetic tape broke…I got so scared
That I didn't dare go back to work
My wife said, "What's the big deal"
With the video-player in hand, she dragged me along
To a technician's house and told her what happened
That technician, whom we called Sister Jin,
Poked fun at me: "What a worrywart"
In no time she spliced the tape as good as new
My wife poked fun at me: "As big as a camel, but short on guts"
After that, I was a bit afraid of my wife

MACHO GAL—STONES

Wifey Series #19

In the late 1980s
In my home district
Korean-style weddings were in demand
But the Korean department store
Where my wife worked
Had no channels for getting merchandise
It was time for me to show what I could do
I had a classmate in Tumen [1]
I got in touch with him by phone
We got things arranged…at the end he told me
To take along a tough guy
But the tough guy turned out to be
A troublemaker…before the shipment was made
He stirred up a dispute with the supplier
We had to have a sit-down…luckily my classmate
Had a lot of pull, so nothing serious happened

"Your old lady is one helluva fierce woman
After the negotiation, when we went to the station
I saw her reach into her pants pocket
To empty out the stones she'd been carrying

Wifey Series
#19

We asked why…Your old lady said
'If there really was going to be a fight
I wanted to have a stone in my hand'"

From that time on, let me tell you
I was thoroughly afraid of my wife

[1] Tumen is a city in eastern Jilin Province.

IF YOU'VE BEEN DRINKING, DON'T COME

Wifey Series #20

On January 12, 2018
I got a big scare
My daughter, who had taken my wife for a checkup
Phoned me and said, "Mom had to go to the hospital"
"Hmm? What is it?"
"It's a laterally spreading tumor
She went straight into surgery. They put on four clamps
To stop the blood. She can't be moved"
"Well, can I go over a little later?"
"Mom says don't come if you've been drinking"
"I have several clients here. How can I not drink?"
"Mom says she's used to the liquor smell
But it will affect other people who are resting"
"But what if your mom gets mad at me?"
"Mom mentioned that…she'll judge by how you make amends
Anyway, don't come if you've been drinking
As for how you'll make amends…
She wants you to hand over the payments for what you publish"

MACHO GAL—LEVEL 3 ELECTRICIAN

Wifey Series
#21

My old lady was sent down to a village…she has done farm work
She's in charge of growing flowers and plants at our house
My old lady has a machinist's certificate
She's in charge of sharpening knives and cutting wood
My old lady is a level 3 electrician
She's in charge of plumbing and electricity at our house
My old lady once worked as a switchboard operator
She's in charge of external communications at our house
My old lady was once a top department store clerk
She's in charge of buying miscellaneous items at our house

REQUESTS FOR CALLIGRAPHY

Wifey Series #22

My old lady only asked me for calligraphy twice

Once when my daughter was in preschool

After my wife had folded covers for the textbooks

She asked me to write the titles

The other time

Was when she founded a dance troupe

"Red Star Dance Troupe"

FIRST ATTEMPT AT DOING BUSINESS

Wifey Series #23

In 1987, my wife's factory was not breaking even
She was laid off for a few months
This wouldn't do…she had to find a way
To earn back her lost wages
So she decided to bake pastries for sale
After some failed attempts…she went through a friend
To contact someone in Ningvan who made a living from pastries
Watching him go through it once, she was able to master it

Now that she knew how to bake cakes, it was time to sell them
That happened to be during rice-planting season
I took time on a weekend to go with my old lady
We took some freshly made cakes to Dage Village
Where we planned to sell them beside paddy fields

In order to sell them, we had to give people a taste
But as my wife watched the cake tasters licking their lips
She felt embarrassed about selling them
"Let's just divvy them up among the people
We have ties with all of these country people"
My old lady was blinking her eyes as she said this

Wifey Series
#23

"I don't see a problem. Go right ahead."
My wife flashed me a wisp of a smile
Hopping like a little bird, with the cakes in her arms
She handed them out door-to-door, happy as you please

It seemed that neither of us was cut out
For doing business…the next morning
While lying under the covers she said
"Well, this attempt at business has gone sour [1]
This bears out the saying…
We'"raided the hen's nest but ended up breaking the eggs!'"

[1] In the local dialect of Jilin Province, the Chinese word for "go sour" is HUANG-LE, which literally means "turn yellow." This yellowness fits amusingly with color of eggs used in making a cake.

THE FIRST ACCORDION

Wifey Series #24

After the Chaoxian Minority came to Tianjin
Due to problems of language and household registry
It was not easy for the children to attend school
My classmate in Tianjin
Set up a private school…he asked my old lady to help
He wasn't asking for much…just to solicit donations
My wife was new in Tianjin…didn't know any bosses
My classmate gave her addresses of some company bosses
My old lady took a co-worker along with her
When they met a boss, my wife got straight to the point
She talked about the function of Chaoxian Minority schools
Then went on to the importance of education

"If it's not convenient to give money
You can donate useful items
For instance, the kids don't have an accordion yet
You can buy one on credit from a Korean enterprise"

In this way
My old lady obtained the school's first batch
Of Wutai Brand accordions

FIVE HUNDRED YUAN PER MONTH   Wifey Series #25

My old lady doesn't believe in Buddhism or Daoism
She doesn't believe in Jesus either...but while
   she was helping my classmate
She went to church every week, with a bible
Under her arm...sang the hymns and prayed earnestly
Every month the school got a donation of 500 yuan
From the church...The only condition
Was that my old lady would keep going to church

CONFIDENCE IN HER OWN JUDGEMENT

Wifey Series #26

We moved house more times in 1987
Than in any other year
From March to November
We moved seven times

Watching my mate's slim figure from behind
As she carried boxes into our new place
In my heart I felt unworthy

"I'm really sorry about this
I hope the apartment is not disappointing"

"Not at all. Why would it be?"

"Hmm? Do you have that much confidence in me?"

"Of course I have confidence
But it is not in you
I have confidence in my own judgement"

TO COOK YOUR MEALS

Wifey Series
#27

One day in 2007
My old lady suddenly phoned me
Said she'd be coming home

"I have things all arranged at the factory
And I've bought a ticket for this evening"

I said, "We haven't even talked it over
In January of '93, when I first went into business, it was the same
I told you to wait for word from me
But on the third day after I got to Harbin
You showed up along with our child
In June of '93 when I went to Tianjin, it was the same
I told you to wait for me to settle in, then come
But on the fifth day after I got to Tianjin
You showed up along with the child
You could have been earning money. What was the point?"

"There was no need to talk it over
I didn't care about earning money or not
I just wanted to come back
To cook your meals"

YOU DON'T OBJECT, DO YOU?

Wifey Series
#28

Getting home from work, before I even removed my shoes
My old lady fired off this sentence:

"Big Auntie [your oldest sister] says your younger brother is sick"
"I know…Didn't I already wire her some money?"

"That's not what I'm talking about…your brother can't
    stay with her in Tianjin
He wants to recuperate at Second Auntie's place in Xiangshui"

My brother has serious rheumatism
He has a hard time walking
When it flares up, he can't get around at all

"Well, what can we do?…Neither of us can go
So we'll have to trouble Second Sister with this"

"That's what I wanted to tell you…we can't go
Even if we went, we couldn't stay long
So I went ahead and wired money to Second Auntie today
You don't have any objections, do you?"

PHONE CONTACTS

Wifey Series #29

In my list of contacts in my cell phone
The nickname given to my wife has always been specified by her
At the beginning of last year she suddenly informed me
"Change my name in your contacts list to 'Helpmate'"
(previously it had been "Beloved Wife")
"Uh…What about my nickname in your contacts list?"
"No need to concern yourself. Why is that?
I am in charge of my name in your contacts list
I'm also in charge of your name in my contacts list
What of it? Do you think differently?"
"No, no" I quickly changed my old lady's nickname
To "Helpmate" in my contacts list
Then in a mild voice I explained
"I was just making sure, is that OK?"

"A BIG GUY"

Wifey Series
#30

One day my old lady was in an extra good mood
She pulled out her cell phone and said
"Look at the address book in my phone
Do you know what you're called?"
I looked: I am called "A Big Guy"
"'A Big Guy'…'A Big Guy'?
That's a name for someone in the underworld, isn't it?
This doesn't look right…not right
You have 'A Big Guy,' so don't tell me
You have 'B Big Guy,' 'C Big Guy' or 'N Big Guy'?"
My old lady bopped me on the head
"You're thinking in the wrong direction again
I put 'A' in front of your name
Don't you see…this way it will pop up first?"
I grabbed her phone for a look
A Baby
A Big Guy1
A Big Guy2
A Big Guy Bank Card

DIARY

Wifey Series
#31

My old lady has a good traditional habit
She keeps a diary…writes in it daily
Never misses a day, 365 days a year
Her daily entry is just a few lines long
She writes large characters, so her daily entry
Is usually no longer than 50 words
(I don't have a diary-writing habit
Now and then I write an entry in my .qq space)

"September 2011, Week 37
September 3rd event, gave 100 yuan
Normal softball lesson, but A and B did not cooperate
In a small collective, we don't want a split
…
The past three years, what has happened
Is what I'm most unwilling to see
How could the person closest to A and B
Behave in the worst possible way?:
Today, nine people went to rehearse at the hospital:
Eleven people formally took part in our sports event:
At 12 o'clock I led A and B in a three-person meeting"

"September 2011, week 39

12th

Spent Mid-Autumn Festival at home by myself

…

15th

Today A and B started to pair up

My mood is improving…very happy

THE THOUSAND-CHARACTER CLASSIC

Wifey Series #32

In 2013…Some kind of bee got under my old lady's bonnet
Maybe it was a breakthrough in her personal growth
That was right after the New Year's Day festivities
I was still in an alcohol haze…not fully awake
She fired a question at me:
"How many books do you read in a year?"
"That doesn't seem to have anything to do with you"
"This year it does, because…
I…want…to…make…money!"
"Mm-hmm, and how will you do that?"
"We two will make a bet"…"Well, what will we bet on?"
"First you say if you'll agree to a bet or not"
"What's to be afraid of…Aside from quitting liquor and tobacco
I fear nothing…I agree to whatever it is"
"Tell you what…by year's end, I'll memorize
   the Thousand Character Classic
And you read one hundred books
If you lose, you'll forfeit a whole year of living expenses
I'll forfeit five Yuan for each character I fall short"

After she memorized 120-some lines

Wifey Series
#32

And I read 70-some books

My old lady said, "I'll let you go this year

What with national, provincial and city contests, I'm busy"

CHOPPING KNIFE

Wifey Series #33

My old lady has a husky voice, like a man's
Over the phone, people address her
As "Buddy," "Sir" or "Brother"

While we were living in Qingdao, once I went outside
In the company of my wife and daughter
People gave us strange glances
As if wanting to keep out of our way

I asked what this was all about
My wife just smiled and chortled
My daughter had to hold her belly from laughing. She said

"A few days ago, I went with Mom to a variety store
The clerk there had a bad attitude
So Mom wife walked over to the store next door
'Do you have a chopping knife?'…She just wanted to switch
From one store to another, but she spoke in such a mannish voice
The manager of the store was dumbfounded
He just looked at her, not daring to speak"

Wifey Series
#33

Since then, within the radius of a few bus stops from home
My wife has a swagger in her walk

RESUMÉ

Wifey Series
#34

My old lady's resumé is very simple

She was born in Qingdao
Sole daughter of a military family
Later followed her parents to reside in Ning'an
From grades 1 through 9 went to Chaoxian Minority schools…
    learned to dance
After graduating, she heeded the summons
Went down to the countryside, worked in a "celebrity village" [1]
Ten kilometers from the county seat, a Chaoxian ethnic village
In her collective…she saw a teen-aged girl
Subjected to critique for having a love affair
At a village assembly saw a pretty young woman
Get her head shaved for being a "worn-out slipper"
In 1979 tested into a technician's school…county level
After graduating, worked at a fertilizer plant…county level
Worked as milling machine operator, electrician,
    switchboard operator
Later her brother wanted to change his job category
She switched jobs with him…went to a
    Chaoxian Minority department store

Then in a careless moment she got married to me
An airy-headed bookworm…we tested
   the waters of business…took a buyout
First in Tianjin, then Harbin…became a clothing vendor
Opened a Korean restaurant in Qingdao…first in the city
Ran an employment agency…best in Qingdao
Set up a factory in Rushan…thirty workers
Then she followed me to Jilin…got involved in plaza dancing
Right up to today…now she's in late middle age

My old lady's resumé is very simple
Not as complicated as mine…in 5-point type
Mine takes up over three A4 pages

---

[1] A "celebrity village" is an exemplary village which is frequently written about in government media reports. It is frequently visited by officials and reporters.

RADIUS OF ACTIVITY

Wifey Series #35

My old lady has a small radius of activity

Except for trips to training sessions and contests

Her movements can be described as "three points, two lines"

House——dance studio——plaza

The dance studio could be in Jiangnan

Or it could be in Jiangbei

The plaza could be in Tiedong district

Or it could be in Jiangxi [1]

Sometimes it could even be in a theater

Or it could be in a shopping center near the Natatorium

Wherever it may be, her movements can be described

As "three points, two lines"

[1] "Jiangnan," "Jiangbei," "Tiedong" and "Jiangxi" are districts in Jilin City. The meanings of their names are as follows: "South-of-River," "North-of-River," "East-of-Railway" and "West-of-River."

Wifey Series
#36

That when an enterprise changes hands and buys out workers
They can sign up for unemployment insurance

After that, she couldn't get over what had happened...
From then on, each year on Tomb Sweeping Day
And on 30th day of the New Year, she would buy joss paper
Write her parents' names in the circles, also my older brother
Along with her younger brother

LIFE EXPERIENCE

Wifey Series #38

My old lady has seen a great deal of the world

She has taken part in three national contests
Softball…matron-level
She has taken part in three national training programs
Public fitness…all expenses paid
Attended three annual national meetings in Korea
"Korea Insurance and Investment Association"…elite level
Won gold, silver, bronze medals…
    provincial performance competitions
Her travels have covered the northeast provinces…
Ventured into Hong Kong, Shenzhen, Macau…
    made ocean crossings…
Left footprints across these vast mountains and
    rivers as beautiful as brocade
And she has never been defeated (to sum things up)

One night, talking to herself
My old lady, who has such rich life experience, said:
"Only America, Europe and Japan remain unconquered"

ON CARING FOR OUR HEALTH

Wifey Series
#39

Ever since WeChat became popular
My old lady has emphasized health
Stinky bean curd—not supposed to eat it
Preserved fruits—not supposed to eat them
Salt-dried greens—not supposed to eat them
Pickled vegetables—not supposed to eat them
Dried bean curd—not supposed to eat it
Fried sesame twists—not supposed to eat them
Broiled meats—not supposed to eat them

I said, "From the way they talk
Chinese people would have gone extinct
Long ago…How could they have survived?"

There's a grain of truth, but we need to see evidence
You use Baidu and Sohu and Google
But they won't tell you
They don't lead you to our daughter
The most knowledgeable person in our household

My daughter said, "It's a matter of daily intake

Wifey Series
#39

They don't mention dosage…and besides

Nobody eats just one thing

Things are eaten with other things that neutralize them"

After that…there was no after that

SOMETHING THAT BOTHERS ME   Wifey Series #40

It's not that she forces me every evening
To wash my feet and brush my teeth
The hardest thing to take
Is being made to eat honey every morning

In the past my mother told me a folk saying:
"Eat honey for two days and you'll get sick of it"
I didn't believe that at all
How could a person get tired of eating honey?

But now I believe it
Not just at every meal, even three days in a row
Is enough to make you sick of it

MY OLD LADY CARRIED ME ON HER BACK

Wifey Series #41

In 1986 I was only a hair's breadth away
From giving up the ghost, due to hemorrhagic fever

At the beginning I didn't know
Thought I had caught a cold or a stomach bug
I took cold remedies and got an injection
Nothing I tried made it better

It even seemed that I saw a ghost
My old lady said we should go to the hospital, get it looked at
I thought I could suffer through it until I got better
But I didn't even have strength
To lift a finger

My old lady said this won't do
You have to go to the hospital
But I couldn't even get up
Our brick bed was a few meters from the door
From there to the intersection was ten more meters
But I couldn't get out of bed
Couldn't take a step

Wifey Series
#41

My old lady said this won't do
There was no other way but for her
To prop me against the wall
Then turn around and load me onto her back
She carried me to the road and hailed a pedicab
My old lady is 158 centimeters tall
I am 178 centimeters

MACHO GAL—FACTORY

Wifey Series #42

In 2007, my old lady said
She couldn't keep going at the employment agency
She wanted to switch trades, get into processing raw materials
I said, "See what you can do on your own
I don't know about processing raw materials"

When I went to see her at year's end
My old lady was already at Ru-shan
She had recruited 30-some workers
The factory was running like a ball of fire
Mother-in-law, Younger Uncle
My younger brother and his wife
The whole crew was supported by my old lady

BOSS IN THE YEARS 2000 AND 2002

Wifey Series
#43

I went through two bouts of hepatitis A,
    with only a year between them
I entered the hospital and was kept there for two months
My salary was only 700 yuan, and my two hospital stays
Cost around 20,000 yuan each, but I couldn't work
So my wages were docked. My hospital bills
Were paid by my old lady; every few days
She would send me 800 or 1000 yuan
In the end, when I had almost recovered
The payments fell behind; my drug regimen was interrupted
This led to a 12-day extension of my stay
My wife phoned the hospital staff
I heard her voice through the receiver
Speaking sobbingly on the other end:
"It's my fault…for not keeping up with the payments"

WATCH OVER ME

Wifey Series #44

Because my old lady was in Qingdao
When my daughter took entrance exams in 2004
And tested into Qingdao University
My old lady said:
"I had planned to go back to Jilin in 2004
But I'll continue to live in Qingdao
To take care of our daughter
On one hand I'll earn money for her tuition
On the other hand I'll support my old man"
From 2000 to 2007
Our three-person-household
Was supported by my wife

FIRST PIECE OF JEWELRY

Wifey Series
#45

On July 12th of 1993
At last I received my first monthly salary
For working at a Korean enterprise
1629 yuan
In my hand I was holding the most money
I had ever held at one time
Grabbing my old lady's slender hand
Like a streak of smoke, I zoomed
Downtown to Tianjin Guomao Building
Straight to a jewelry counter
Wanting to buy her the first piece of jewelry
Since we two had met
My old lady said, "Not right now"
Let's put some aside…It's good to save"
A moment later she looked up
I broke my silence, as if making a hard decision, and said:
"Then let's buy a necklace"
On the way home
My old lady raised her head, looked into my face and said:
"When I insisted that we shouldn't buy it
Did that make you sad?"

ASKING FOR AN EVENING OFF

Wifey Series #46

It was totally unexpected, in the first month of 2018
My old lady, of all people,
Was hospitalized for surgery
It so happened that January 13th was the date
Of the Jilin City Chaoxian Minority New Year Talent Show
A troupe from Mudan River Chaoxian Arts Hall
Had been invited to come and perform
But I couldn't get the evening free
With a hangdog expression I asked my old lady to let me off
"I'm sorry sweetheart, I can't get free
So let me have the evening off, alright?"
My old lady said:
"You should put priority on your career; that's alright
Just don't embarrass yourself by getting drunk and falling asleep
Even so, you'll have to be penalized
You'll have to cough up my living expenses
One hundred yuan a day while I'm in the hospital"

LIVING ON RICE PORRIGE

Wifey Series
#47

My wife's hospitalization in January 2018
Was her longest hospital stay
Since she and I got married
(Except for when she gave birth to our daughter)
She stayed in the hospital for three days
When she was released the doctor instructed her
She should not carelessly eat
Green vegetables…fish and meat pickles
She also should not eat
Steamed rice or noodle dishes
She can only eat rice porridge
For one month she is not allowed
To out outdoors or take exercise
Yesterday night my old lady stood on the scales
Looking a bit disconsolate, and said:
"I've lost three jin, and I won't be able
To take part in tomorrow's performance"

TAOBAO

Wifey Series #48

My old lady likes the online shopping site Taobao
Whether something is useful or not
If it strikes her fancy, she hits the button
From clothes to kitchen utensils
The most successful time was when
She bought a traditional scholar's robe for me
The worst fiasco was when
She bought for herself
A dance outfit that looked like shish-kabob

NOW THEY ARE MAKING DEMANDS

Wifey Series #49

A few years ago

My old lady rounded up a few middle-aged mamas

Together they founded a dance troupe

They called it "Red Star Dance Troupe"

In the past, as long as they could go onstage

They would participate in any activity

At some events, organizers even asked for a meal fee

Even so, my old lady would lead her troupe

To take part in the performance

Sometimes they would take lunch bags

If the venue provided lunch

They would feel extra lucky

But now

Times have changed

The quality of middle-aged women dancers

Has been raised to a new level

Now they are making demands

When invited to put on two acts at an event

If the performance payment is under 100 yuan

They won't accept

VOLUNTEER

Wifey Series
#50

Last year

The City Cultural Bureau

Was recruiting cultural volunteers

My old lady was in Beijing for a training class

(in social fitness)

So she didn't sign up

After coming home she had a blow-up

"Why didn't you sign up for me?"

I said, "You're already a state-certified public fitness coach

Do you really need to be a volunteer too?"

My old lady said:

"A coach is a coach

A volunteer is a volunteer

You can't lump them together

It's the duty of every citizen

To take part in volunteer activities"

Beginning the next day

She scurried about, filled out retractive paperwork

And at last succeeded in becoming

A Jilin City cultural volunteer

That evening she came home looking happy

Wifey Series
#50

Like a teen-age girl
Who was falling in love

SECOND MENOPAUSE

Wifey Series
#51

I am afraid to hear my old lady speak of her menopause

My old lady's menopause

Was especially long

All-in-all it lasted ten years

From age 45 or 46

Until age 55 or 56

It didn't end until early last year

I let out a long breath

It was finally over

I grew bolder at home

Started to speak in a louder voice

One day we ate at a Korean restaurant on Quanluo Avenue

When we were half-done eating

My wife uttered

The scariest thing I have heard

Since we got married:

"I think I'm going to have

A second menopause"

She dragged out the last syllable like a Peking opera singer

That frightened me so much

I don't dare to speak loudly anymore

RETAIL VENDING

Wifey Series
#52

In 1996, at the Harbin Train Station
We sold wholesale-priced clothes in the basement mall
Business was not good…sales were limited
My old lady proceeded to carve out a new market
She did retail sales at high-end department stores
Such as Harbin First and Songlei
Also in the basement of Guomao and at Yonghua Mall
Once I went with my old lady
To settle accounts at Songlei…the bookkeeper said:
"In Songlei Mall, you got back your investment
Sooner than any other vendor
And your sales volume was biggest
It comes to 50,000 yuan."
My old lady was still dissatisfied
As she riffled through wads of cash
She said, "The profit is too low"

FILING A LAWSUIT

Wifey Series #53

During the three-year period
That we did business in Harbin
My old lady filed one lawsuit
It was not for a large sum
Only 30,000 or 40,000 yuan
I said, "After you pay the lawyer's fee
And the compulsory enforcement fee
Hardly anything will be left. Don't bother…"
My old lady said: "I want to file this suit, no matter what"
That woman knows it's a small amount…so she thinks
   she can get away with it
She may famous as a flimflammer in our basement mall
But I want to sue her anyway; I want to make her lose face"
Thus the protracted case made its way through the courts
My wife's lawsuit won in the first hearing.
   The second hearing reached a verdict:
Compulsory enforcement against the defendant
   within 20 days
After paying the fees, my old lady was left with 5000 yuan
This was a big loss of face for the defendant, so soon after
She removed her booth from the basement mall

Wifey Series
#53

My old lady shook her bobbed hairdo
"Hmph! That was the effect I wanted!' [1]

[1] The poet's wife had rented retail space and a counter in the basement mall for a two-year period. The "flimflammer" occupied the space and took away the sales counter while the contract was still in effect. The poet's wife sued to recover her rental payment.

KOREAN RESTAURANT

Wifey Series #54

We spent the New Year of 2000 in Qingdao
Acting on behalf of a Korean businessman
My old lady opened a Korean restaurant
She gave it the name "Korean Eatery"
Business was not bad, a few thousand Yuan per day
After New Year's Day I went back to work in Jilin
Right after the Fifteenth I got a call
My wife and the owner did not see eye to eye
So she ended up withdrawing
The owner, seeing how good business was
Suspected my old lady of filling her own pocket
Which angered her so much she resigned
Right around that time, Junzhi introduced her
To a job at an employment agency
My old lady looked into it: this was a business opportunity
She didn't ask for the job, but she went ahead
And opened an employment agency herself

EMPLOYMENT AGENCY

Wifey Series
#55

In the year 2000, most of the employment agencies in Qingdao
That served members of the Chaoxian Minority
Were clustered at Li Village Market
Those employment agencies gave referrals
To Chaoxian folks who came to Qingdao seeking work
They were also a source of labor
For Korean businesses that needed Chaoxian employees
My old lady saw that the referral agencies charged too much
So she came up with a method
Of providing lifelong service
After payment was made for the first referral
Subsequent referrals would be done for free
In this way
Her job referral business was growing like a house afire
Within a couple of months, other referral agencies
Come looking for my old lady
They said she was undermining the rules of the trade
She was influencing the business of other agencies
My old lady said:
"Each agency should mind its own business,
    not interfere with others

Wifey Series
#55

If we want to reach a consensus

It would be best to set up an 'employment agency association'

To protect the interests of fellow tradesmen"

Before long

The first Employment Agency Association

Was established in Qingdao

My old lady was named secretary-in-chief

WHO FIRED WHOM?

Wifey Series
#56

My old lady has been involved with many Korean enterprises
For the most part she has held posts at the managerial level
In the year 2006
My old lady came close to earning big money
My old lady phoned me to say
It was easy to make money on a certain kind of transaction
She said it had to do with name-brand apparel
For instance Adidas and Nike
There were all kinds of items
The key was to have the supplier's factory
Divert extra lots of merchandise your way
Such products were to a certain extent genuine
But it would only work if they used my old lady's ID
I said, "The earnings are easy, but the risks are high
Whatever you do, don't get me mixed up in this"
The next day, my old lady called, saying
She had resigned from her position. She said:
"I wouldn't want to influence your prospects"
For the past twenty years
For the most part, my old lady has been the one
Who has fired her bosses!

TOO MUCH TO DRINK

Wifey Series
#57

My old lady has seen large sums of money

She can spread her arms to indicate

What a big pile 50,000 in 10-Yuan bills makes

My old lady has drunk big amounts of liquor

The biggest amount was a bottle of 110-proof "Erwo-tou"

And she was able to hail a taxi and come home

Once while lying in bed she said to me

"Have you seen how big 50,000 Yuan is?"

Back then we didn't have hundred-Yuan bills

She used her arms to show me the size

It was as big as a primary student's desk

"It was this b-b-…"

Before she finished saying "big"

She lay back onto the bed

And fell asleep

ADHERING TO A CODE OF LOYALTY

Wifey Series #58

My old lady adheres to a code of loyalty
During our time in Tianjin my old lady worked
As manager and treasurer in a Korean enterprise
One day Junzhi showed up with his head shaved
And a bandage on his forehead
My old lady jumped to her feet
Asked him what was the matter
Junzhi said that the soup was rancid this morning
But nobody dared to mention it. This made Junzhi so angry
He went to the boss and demanded to know
Why rancid soup was being served to workers
The boss flew into a rage
Smacked a soup bowl against Junzhi's forehead
Hearing this, my old lady flew into a rage
She went right out and called together
Her Third Uncle and her niece's boyfriend
They hailed a cab straight for Junzhi's company
To have a showdown with that boss…
They raised an outcry and my wife vowed
Such an affront to her female dignity would be avenged
They made such a scene in front of that Korean boss

Wifey Series
#58

He acquiescently forked over medical fees and compensation
He also requested my company's boss
To come forward and smooth things over
Afterward my old lady said:
"If I want to curse Junzhi, I'll curse him every day
If I want to hit Junzhi, I'll hit him every day
That's my business, but I won't allow
Anyone else to get away with it"
Then she wagged her finger at my nose, saying;
"Not you either, buster!"

OLD LADY, LET ME SAY THIS SLOWLY

Wifey Series
#59

Old Lady

The two of us

Are slowly growing old

If it is alright

Old Lady

I am saying that if

It is alright with you

I want to hold

Your slender left hand

And walk together

To keep walking onward

Until the moment

When life's fire burns out

Old Lady

The two of us

Are slowly growing old

But in my eyes

I do not see

So much as a wrinkle

What fills my eyes

Wifey Series
#59

Are the pistils of a lily

Old Lady
Some say that once middle age has passed
We can no longer say that a youthful blush
Still lingers on a coy matron's face
Then why
Are my eyes still greeted
By the curiosity and vitality
Of a young girl?

Old Lady
If it should happen
I'm saying that if
It should ever happen
When the day comes
That our life-force is used up
And one of us
Has to depart before the other
Then my wish
Is to let you go first

Wifey Series
#59

I don't want to make you
Pass your waning days
In heart-wrenching grief

Old Lady
If it has to happen
I am saying that if
It has to happen
If I must depart before you
Then it is my wish
That your memories will fade
It is my wish
That you pass your remaining years
Free of grief and disturbance
Rather than letting you pass
The twilight of your years
In solitude and endless loneliness

Old Lady
That day you asked
You asked if I want

Wifey Series #59

To marry you in the next lifetime
You said:
"I don't want the illusion
Of lifetime after lifetime
Just the actuality of one more lifetime
The next lifetime will be enough"
Old Lady
In the next life, of course
I want to marry you
But if it so happens
I am saying that if
We two are parted
Old Lady
I will hack through thorny thickets to find you
I will cross deserts and grasslands and snowy mountains
If that's what is necessary to find you
I'll seek you from daybreak to twilight
From twilight until daybreak
From my time of birth
Until life's end
Not stopping until I see you

Wifey Series #59

Growing white-haired by my side

Old Lady

If it's alright

I am saying

If it's alright with you

My wish for the next lifetime

Is that your parents and my parents

Will be neighbors

We will share childhood games

Watch over each other through life

Never to be parted

Until our loving bond

Is air-dried

Unchanging and ageless

AFTERWORD

I've put in half a month
For the sake of my old lady
Verbalizing these slices of life
From the times we've gone through

As I tap on the keyboard
Lamplight cast upon the screen
Wavers and transforms
To a catkin-sized flame
Belonging to the candle
That burned on our nuptial night
Flickering on the yellowed paper
Of our black-and-white wedding photo

On the screen
My old lady and I
Are slowly growing old
Slowly returning to our origin
Slowly being born anew
Slowly having another go

Jan. 3-Jan. 25, 2018, in Snail Abode, beside Songhua River

www.ingramcontent.com/pod-product-compliance
Lightning Source LLC
Chambersburg PA
CBHW071220070526
44584CB00019B/3084